THE CHEYENNE

A TRUE BOOK

by
Andrew Santella

Children's Press®
A Division of Scholastic Inc.

New York Toronto London Auckland Sydney
Mexico City New Delhi Hong Kong
Danbury, Connecticut

A father and son sell items at a market.

Reading Consultant
Nanci R. Vargus, Ed.D.
*Primary Multiage Teacher
Decatur Township Schools
Indianapolis, IN*

Content Consultant
Ruth J. Krochock, Ph.D.
*Archaeologist
Davis, California*

The photograph on the cover shows Cheyenne children in native dress. The photograph on the title page shows a man wearing a native headdress during Cheyenne Frontier Days.

Library of Congress Cataloging-in-Publication Data

Santella, Andrew.
    The Cheyenne / by Andrew Santella.
        p.   cm. – (A true book)
    Includes bibliographical references and index.
    Summary: Describes the Cheyenne way of life, including their traditions, customs, buffalo hunts, leaders, and land.
    ISBN 0-516-22502-2 (lib. bdg.)   0-516-26974-7 (pbk.)
    1. Cheyenne Indians—History—Juvenile literature. 2. Cheyenne Indians—Social life and customs—Juvenile literature. [1. Cheyenne Indians. 2. Indians of North America—Great Plains.] I. Title. II. Series.
E99.C53 S74 2002
978.004'973—dc21   2001032297

1 2 3 4 5 6 7 8 9 10 R 11 10 09 08 07 06 05 04 03 02

Contents

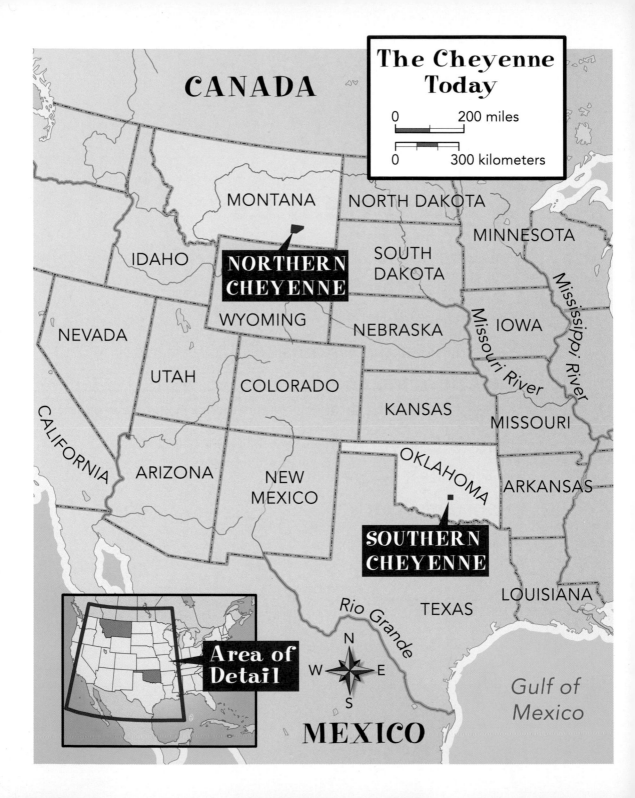

The Cheyenne Today

0 — 200 miles
0 — 300 kilometers

CANADA

MONTANA   NORTH DAKOTA

MINNESOTA

IDAHO

SOUTH
DAKOTA

NORTHERN
CHEYENNE

WYOMING   NEBRASKA

IOWA

Missouri River

Mississippi River

NEVADA

UTAH   COLORADO

KANSAS

MISSOURI

CALIFORNIA

ARIZONA

NEW
MEXICO

OKLAHOMA

ARKANSAS

SOUTHERN
CHEYENNE

LOUISIANA

Rio Grande   TEXAS

Area of
Detail

N
W   E
S

MEXICO

Gulf of
Mexico

The Cheyenne and Horses

Hundreds of years ago, the Cheyenne lived on the banks of the Minnesota River. They were peaceful people who seldom traveled far from their villages. They built homes made of wood frames covered with sod, which is a layer of grass and dirt. They ate small animals and fish. They also gathered roots and berries from the fields.

Around the year 1700, the Cheyenne way of life began to change. First, more warlike groups arrived in the area and forced them to move west. The Cheyenne moved into what is now North Dakota and settled in new villages. There they became farmers and planted corn, beans, squash, and other crops.

Even in their new home the Cheyenne were still not safe

As the Cheyenne moved west, they began planting crops such as corn.

from **raids** by other tribes. Larger tribes attacked the Cheyenne again and again. Finally, the few surviving Cheyenne decided to move again. This time they turned south, toward the Black Hills of South Dakota.

Shortly after they moved south, something happened that made life much better for the Cheyenne. Sometime around 1740, the Cheyenne acquired horses from neighboring tribes. These horses were **descendants** of the first horses brought to North America by Spanish explorers. In a short time, the Cheyenne became excellent horse riders.

Their skill on horseback helped the Cheyenne develop a new way of life based on roaming the Great Plains. On horseback, they

The Cheyenne quickly learned to train and ride horses (above). Horses remain valuable to the Cheyenne today.

were able to travel long distances to trade with other tribes. They were able to follow and hunt the great buffalo herds. And on horseback, Cheyenne warriors became very powerful.

Hunting on the Plains

The Cheyenne learned to use their horses to become great hunters. They learned to ride their horses even without using their hands. Because of this skill, they were able to use a bow and arrow while riding. Before they had horses, the Cheyenne hunted buffalo on

Before they had horses, the Cheyenne had to invent clever ways to hunt on foot.

foot. They formed large hunting parties that tried to surround buffalo herds, so that they could be trapped and killed.

On horseback, it only took one hunter to chase and kill a buffalo.

On horseback, a single
Cheyenne hunter could chase
down buffalo one by one. As
he caught them, he could kill

them using his bow and arrow or a spear.

The buffalo hunt became a central part of Cheyenne life. The Cheyenne found ways to use every part of the buffalo they killed, and didn't waste a thing. Buffalo meat provided food. The bones of the buffalo were carved into tools used for sewing. Buffalo hide could be made into leather for ropes. The Cheyenne even used buffalo hide to make their homes.

A woman stretches and dries a buffalo hide.

Once the Cheyenne moved to the Great Plains, they began living in tepees. These were cone-shaped structures made of wooden poles. Cheyenne women stitched together ten to twenty buffalo hides and stretched them across the poles to make walls. With this simple design, tepees were easy to set

A tepee is made by stretching buffalo hides over wooden poles.

Lightweight tepees allowed the Cheyenne to easily move their homes from place to place.

up and take down. Cheyenne women could set up a tepee in a matter of hours. These easy-to-make homes were perfect because the Cheyenne did not stay in one place for very long. With their herds of horses and their light tepees, the Cheyenne were able to roam across the plains to find the best hunting grounds.

Cheyenne Warriors

Horses helped the Cheyenne become feared warriors. By the time they were twelve years old, Cheyenne boys learned to ride horses and to handle weapons. Warriors did battle with other tribes in order to take their best horses. One of the best ways for a warrior to prove his bravery

Cheyenne boys were taught to ride horses at a young age.

was to raid another tribe for its horses. The Cheyenne did not consider this a crime. They considered horse-raiding a great skill. The ability to take horses from other tribes earned a Cheyenne warrior great honor.

A Cheyenne warrior holds a stick for counting coup.

Another way to earn honor was to strike an enemy warrior with a long stick. This skill was called counting coup. Counting coups earned a warrior the respect of the whole tribe.

Even some Cheyenne women became warriors. They were called Manly Hearted Women and they took part in buffalo hunts and fought in battles.

The Cheyenne formed five military societies to celebrate the skills of their warriors. They were called Fox, Elk, Dog, Shield, and Bowstring. One of the societies, the Dog Soldiers, became famous for their fierce battles with the United States Army in the 1800s.

Traditions and Customs

Each June, the Cheyenne performed one of their most important **rituals**—the Renewal of the **Sacred** Arrows. It happened on the solstice, which is the longest day of the year. The entire tribe came together on this day and set up their tepees in a large circle. They

The Cheyenne prepared for the Renewal of the Sacred Arrows ceremony by first moving their tepees into a large circle.

left a small gap between tepees at the north end of the circle. In the very center of this circle, they set up a large

23

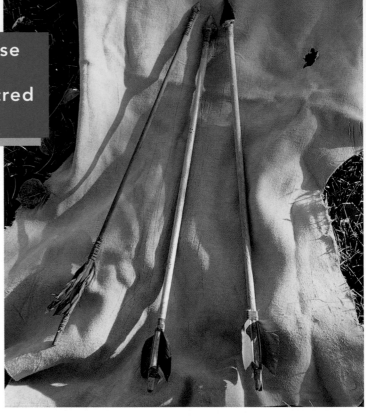

tepee called the Sacred Arrow Lodge. Cheyenne holy men brought a bundle of four arrows into this tepee. The arrows were holy to the Cheyenne. They believed that two of the arrows would give them power to kill buffalo and other animals. They believed that the other two arrows would give them power to defeat their enemies. The Cheyenne practiced the Renewal of the Sacred Arrows because they believed it allowed them to hunt and fight with the arrows successfully.

Another important Cheyenne ritual was the Sun Dance. The Cheyenne believed that the

These two men practiced the Sun Dance to renew the forces of nature.

power of the sun made life possible. In the Sun Dance, they worshipped the power of the sun. They believed that if they performed the Sun Dance, they would receive all the natural things they needed to live. They believed that as long as they performed the Sun Dance, water and wild animals would always be available to them.

The Sun Dance lasted for eight days. During this time the Cheyenne sang, offered prayers, and danced around a pole set up at the center of a special Sun Dance lodge. While they were dancing, the Cheyenne would blow on

Sun Dance rattle and eagle bone whistle

whistles made of eagle bones. Some Cheyenne men performed very painful dances of their own that demonstrated their bravery. In these dances, they might not eat or drink for several days.

Women also played important roles in Cheyenne society. They made shirts, leggings, and robes for their families to wear. Some

This woman is preparing buffalo hides to be made into clothing.

Cheyenne women prepare food for the family.

women belonged to special clubs that sewed fancy clothes. Other groups of women made **moccasins**. Older women also helped bring young Cheyenne men and women together in marriage. A man did not directly ask a woman to marry him. Instead, he sent older female relatives to bring gifts to the family of the woman he wanted to marry. Only then could the marriage be arranged.

The Cheyenne and the United States

In the 1820s, more and more white settlers began moving across the Great Plains. One group of Cheyenne moved south so they could trade with settlers heading west along wagon trails. These Cheyenne settled along the Arkansas

Many white settlers traveled across the Great Plains in the early 1800s (left). Some Cheyenne moved south to trade with the settlers (below).

River in what is now southern Colorado. Around the same time, another group of Cheyenne moved west from the Black Hills. They settled in what is now Wyoming and Montana. The first group came to be called the Southern Cheyenne. The second group was known as the Northern Cheyenne.

None of the Cheyenne was prepared for the changes that the white settlers brought. Wagon trains filled with settlers frequently rolled through the Plains. Their presence changed the Cheyenne way of life. The Cheyenne depended on buffalo for their existence, but the

Many settlers drove their wagons through the Cheyenne homeland on their way out west (above). Encounters between the settlers and the American Indians sometimes became violent (left).

whites hunted buffalo until they were almost **extinct**.

The Cheyenne signed several treaties with the United States

government in the 1850s and 1860s. None of them lasted very long, however.

Beginning around 1857, the Cheyenne and the U.S. Army fought each other again and again. In 1864, the Cheyenne suffered a terrible **massacre** at the hands of U.S. soldiers. The army launched a surprise attack on a peaceful group of Cheyenne near Sand Creek in Colorado. The soldiers killed hundreds of Cheyenne, including many women and children.

The Cheyenne and the U.S. Army fought frequently in the mid-1800s.

The Sand Creek Massacre only led to more fighting. In 1876, Cheyenne warriors joined in the attack on the U.S. Army at the Battle of Little Big Horn. The warriors killed 225 soldiers commanded by

Lt. Col. George Custer. But the Cheyenne could not resist much longer. They had no choice but to give up their old way of life. They would have to live on **reservations** set up by the United States government.

Ben Nighthorse Campbell

Ben Nighthorse Campbell is a senator and the chairman of the Senate's Indian Affairs Committee.

Northern Cheyenne Ben Nighthorse Campbell is a member of the United States Senate. When he was elected in 1992, he became the first American Indian to be elected to the Senate in more than sixty years. He served in the U.S. Air Force during the Korean War and won a gold medal in judo in the 1963 Pan-American games. He is the chairman of the Senate's Indian Affairs Committee.

Today's Cheyenne

Many of today's Cheyenne live on one of two reservations. About five thousand Southern Cheyenne live on a reservation in Oklahoma. Another three thousand Northern Cheyenne live on a reservation in Montana. In many ways, they live like other Americans. They

A Cheyenne car salesman works out a deal with a customer.

watch the same television programs, eat the same kinds of food, and drive the same cars. But the Cheyenne face their own unique challenges. Some live in poverty, and many

continue to face discrimination.
Many are unable to find jobs
to support their families.

Cheyenne leaders have tried
to help their people get the
education and the jobs they
need. The Southern Cheyenne
operate two casinos on their
Oklahoma reservation. The
casinos provide jobs for
hundreds of Cheyenne. The
Northern Cheyenne operate a
community college so that their
young people have access to

Cheyenne children wear their native dress during the Cheyenne Frontier Days celebration.

higher education. Even as they cherish their traditions, the Cheyenne work toward creating a better future for their people.

To Find Out More

Here are some additional resources to help you learn more about the Cheyenne:

 **Books**

Henry, Christopher A. **Ben Nighthorse Campbell: Cheyenne Chief and U.S. Senator.** Chelsea House, 1994.

Lassieur, Allison. **The Cheyenne.** Bridgestone, 2001.

Sneve, Virginia Driving Hawk. **The Cheyennes.** Holiday House, 1996.